Nita Mehta®

TASTE OF HYDERABAD NON-VEG

Nita Mehta®
B.Sc. (Home Science), M.Sc. (Food and Nutrition)
Gold Medalist

SNAB
Excellence in Books

Nita Mehta®

TASTE OF HYDERABAD NON-VEG

SNAB Excellence in Books

Snab Publishers Pvt Ltd
3A/3, Asaf Ali Road, New Delhi 110 002

Food Styling and Photography by Snab
Typesetting by National Information Technology Academy
3A/3, Asaf Ali Road, New Delhi 110 002

ISBN 978-81-7869-272-2

4th Print 2015

Printed in India at HT Media Limited, Noida

Contributing Writers:
Anurag Mehta
Tanya Mehta
Subhash Mehta

Editors :
Sangeeta
Sunita

Distributed by :
NITA MEHTA BOOKS
3A/3, Asaf Ali Road, New Delhi - 02

Distribution Centre :
D16/1, Okhla Industrial Area, Phase-I,
New Delhi - 110020
Tel.: 26813199, 26813200
E-mail: nitamehta.mehta@gmail.com
Website: www.nitamehta.com

Editorial and Marketing office
E-159, Greater Kailash II, New Delhi 110 048

Recipe Development & Testing:
Nita Mehta Foods - R & D Centre
3A/3, Asaf Ali Road, New Delhi - 110002

Price: Rs. 99/-

Introduction

Hyderabadi food has been popular worldwide and the exotic biryanis have found a place in almost every city of India. But now food-lovers need not look for an eatery for Hyderabadi food. This book provides the original recipes of the cuisine. From snacks to dessert, the best methods have been given, taking care of the non-vegetarian food lovers.

The spices and other ingredients are easily available and all the recipes are simple to follow. Each recipe is detailed and there are tips which make cooking fun.

Surprise your loved ones with the colours, aroma and flavours of Hyderabad.

Nita Mehta

C O N T

Snacks 6

Main Dishes 17

E N T S

SNACKS

Lukhmi

The word lukhmi comes from luqma or morsel. Patties are stuffed with mutton mince. It is a delicacy and is often served as first course or gazak at wedding feasts and other celebrations.

Makes 15-16 *Picture on opposite page*

500 gm mutton mince (*mutton keema*)

1½ tsp salt, 1 tsp red chilli powder, ¼ tsp turmeric powder

2 tsp ginger-garlic paste

½ cup finely chopped green coriander, 5-6 green chillies - chopped

5-6 tbsp lemon juice

3 tbsp oil, oil to fry

DOUGH

2 cups plain flour (*maida*)

1 tsp salt, 5-6 tbsp oil, 2 tbsp yogurt (*dahi*), 1 cup water, approx.

1. Wash mince in a strainer. Cook mince with salt, turmeric, red chilli powder, ginger-garlic paste and ½-¾ cup water. Cover and cook for about 10-15 minutes till mince gets tender.
2. Heat 3 tbsp oil. Add the chopped coriander and green chillies and fry for a minute. Add the boiled mince and cook till it dries completely. Remove from fire. Allow to cool and then add the lemon juice to it. Check salt and add to taste. Keep filling aside.
3. For the dough, add salt, oil and yogurt to the flour and mix well with fingers. Add water, a little at a time, mixing well to get a soft dough. Knead dough till it turns smooth and soft. Put the dough in a polythene bag and refrigerate for half an hour.
4. To make lukhmi, divide the dough into 16 portions. Dusting with a little dry flour, roll it with a rolling pin in an oblong shape of approximately 6" length. Place about 1½ tbsp of the mince on one side. Wet the edges with a little water. Fold over to cover the mince and seal the edges. Trim off the uneven sides with a sharp knife to make a rectangular shaped lukhmi of approximately 3" x 1½" size. Repeat the process with the remaining ingredients.
5. Now heat oil in a kadahi. Deep fry 5-6 lukhmis together on low medium flame till golden brown. Serve hot.

Khorme ke Kebab

Kebabs made from pounded meat. Pounded meat is somewhat stringy and not pasty. Traditionally a pestle and mortar is used for pounding the meat, but if this is not possible, try using a mixer, churning it just a couple of times to avoid the meat from becoming pasty.

Makes 18-20

500 gm boneless mutton - cut into medium pieces

½ tsp ginger paste, 1 tsp garlic paste

¾ tsp salt, or to taste, ½ tsp red chilli powder, ¼ tsp turmeric powder

½ tbsp watermelon seeds (*tarbooz*) & 1 tbsp seeds of musk-melon (*kharbooza*) - ground

¼ cup yogurt - beaten, 60 gm roasted gram (*bhune channe*) - ground to a powder

2 tbsp roughly chopped mint leaves, 2-3 tbsp lemon juice

TO SERVE

2 medium onions, sliced in rings

mint leaves

1. Wash and pat dry mutton. Put in a pressure cooker with salt, red chilli powder, turmeric, ginger and garlic. Add 1½ cups water and pressure cook on high heat to give 3-4 whistles. Reduce heat and keep on fire for 10 minutes. Let the pressure drop by itself.
2. Pound the meat in a mortar with a pestle, taking care that it should not become too pasty and remain somewhat stringy/shredded.
3. Add the yogurt, ground seeds, ground gram, mint leaves and lemon juice to the pounded meat and mix.
4. Take about a tbsp of meat, place it in your palm and roll it oblong into the shape of a sausage - about 2 ¼" size. Repeat the process for the rest of the meat.
5. Deep fry the kebab till golden. Or you can shallow fry the kebabs in a non- stick pan, turning each one until it is golden brown all around. Serve hot, garnished with ringed onions, slices of lemon and mint leaves.

Note

If watermelon and musk-melon seeds are not available, then cashew or almonds or a combination of both may be used as a substitute.

Kursi Miyane

Hard-boiled egg-whites stuffed with mince mixed with boiled yolks. The stuffed whites are sandwiched together and skewered on bamboo sticks, coated with gramflour and fried to perfection.

Makes 6

6 hard-boiled eggs

4-5 tbsp cooked mince (as in *bhuna keema*, recipe on page 52)

½ tsp salt

3-4 tbsp lemon juice

¼ cup chopped green coriander

oil for frying

BATTER

1½ cup besan

½-¾ cup water, approx.

½ tsp red chilli powder

½ tsp salt

1. Boil eggs in 4 cups water with 1 tsp salt for 12-15 minutes. Remove the shell of boiled eggs. Cut the hard-boiled eggs into two. Set aside the halves in pairs. Scoop out the yolks.
2. Mix the yolks with the cooked mince. Add a pinch of salt, lemon juice and the chopped coriander leaves. Divide this mixture into 12 equal portions and use each portion to fill the white of one egg, sandwiching the two halves together. Pierce each egg with a long thin stick to hold the two halves together. Keep aside.
3. Mix besan, salt and red chilli powder in a bowl. Add enough water gradually and mix well to make a smooth batter of thick coating consistency.
4. Heat oil in a kadhai. Dip each egg into the batter, gently shake off the excess batter. Place gently in the hot oil along with the sticks and fry 2-3 pieces at a time, till golden-brown and crisp.

Shikampoor

A kebab, succulent and moist due to the filling of hung yogurt, and yet crisp with chopped onions, and fiery with green chillies.

Makes 24 large kebabs

1 kg boneless mutton, from the leg of goat or lamb, cut into flattish pieces

¼ cup split gram (*channa dal*), 2 onions - roughly chopped

1 tsp ginger paste, 1 tsp garlic paste, 1 tsp salt, 1-½ tsp red chilli powder

1 tsp turmeric powder, 4-5 green chillies - chopped

4-5 tbsp chopped fresh coriander, 1 tbsp chopped mint leaves

GRIND TOGETHER

2 tbsp cashewnuts & 2 tbsp chironji - roasted in a kadhai till light golden

4 cloves (*laung*), 4 green cardamoms (*illaichi*)

1 tsp black cumin seeds (*shah jeera*), 1 tsp peppercorns (*sabut kali mirch*)

FILLING

1 cup yogurt - hang in a muslin cloth for 1 hour, 2 onions - chopped very finely

2-3 green chillies - chopped very finely, 2 tbsp finely chopped mint leaves

1. For filling, hang yogurt in a muslin cloth for all the water to drain off. Mix onions, green chillies and the mint with the hung yogurt. Keep aside.
2. Roast cashewnuts and chironji. Grind together with the given whole spices. Keep powder aside.
3. Heat 6 tbsp oil in a pressure cooker. Put in the mutton, salt and all other ingredients. Add ¾ cup water and pressure cook to give 2-3 whistles. Keep on low heat for 10 minutes. Remove from fire and let the pressure drop by itself.
4. Open the pressure cooker, add the ground spices and nuts and cook stirring constantly till the water dries up. Allow to cool. Then grind to a paste.
5. Take about 2 tbsp of the ground paste and roll it between your palms. Press to flatten a little. Make a dent in the middle with the top of your thumb. Put one tsp of the filling in the hollow space. Fold the sides and seal. A shikampoor should be round and approximately 1½-2" in diameter.
6. Shallow fry the shikampoors, a few at a time in a pan, till golden brown. Serve.

MAIN DISHES

Murgh Malai Korma

A rich, smooth, creamy curry, delicately flavoured with spices.

Serves 6 *Picture on page 17*

800 gm boneless chicken - cut into 1" pieces

4 tomatoes

2 tsp watermelon seeds (*magaz*)

½ cup oil

2 tsp finely chopped, 2 tbsp chopped garlic

2 green chillies - chopped

2 cups yogurt, 1½ cups fresh cream, 1 tsp salt or to taste

GRIND TOGETHER IN A SMALL SPICE GRINDER

10 almonds - chopped

a pinch of grated nutmeg (*jaiphal*), ¼ tsp or a blade of mace (*javetri*)

1 tsp cumin seeds (*jeera*), 1 tsp coriander seeds (*dhania*)

½ tsp peppercorn (*sabut kali mirch*)

2 green cardamoms (*illaichi*) and ½" stick cinnamon (*dalchini*)

1. Boil 3-4 cups water. Put whole tomatoes in boiling water and boil for 3-4 minutes till the skin starts to peel. Remove from water. After they cool down, peel and chop roughly.
2. Grind the tomatoes with watermelon seeds, ginger, garlic, green chillies in a mixer till smooth. Add yogurt to the mixer and blend again to mix the yogurt well with the tomatoes.
3. Heat ½ cup oil in a kadhai and add the prepared tomato-yogurt puree. Stir on medium flame and bring to a boil. Add chicken pieces and salt. Cook without covering on low heat, stirring occasionally till chicken is tender. Add about ¼ cup water if required.
4. When the chicken is tender, add the spices and the almonds ground together. Reduce heat and cook for 2-3 minutes.
5. Add the cream and mix gently. Serve hot.

Lal Mirch ki Machchi

Red chilli fish!

Serves 4

500 gm fish fillets - cut into 2" pieces

6 cloves (*laung*) and seeds of 1 black cardamom (*moti illaichi*) - crushed together

6 dry red chillies, coarsely ground

¼ cup oil, 3 onions - grind to a paste

1 tsp ginger paste, 1½ tsp garlic paste

¼ tsp turmeric powder

½ tsp degi red chilli powder

2-3 tbsp lemon juice, 1 tsp salt

1. Heat oil in a flat pan or a non-stick pan. Add crushed cloves, black cardamom and dry red chillies and cook for a minute. When chillies start to change colour, add the onion paste and cook on medium flame till golden.
2. Add ginger, garlic, salt, turmeric and red chilli powder, cook for a minute. Add about 1 cup of water. Bring to a boil. Reduce heat. Place the fish fillets in the simmering liquid in a single layer. Cover the pan with a lid and cook for 4-5 minutes, stirring occasionally.
3. Remove lid and cook till the gravy gets thick and the fish gets cooked and spices coat the fish. Add lemon juice before serving.

Bhuna Gosht

Roasted meat. This process of stirring & browning the spices & meat is called Bhoon-na. To prevent the spices from sticking to the pan while they are being browned, it is necessary to stir-fry constantly.

Serves 4

½ kg mutton with bones (from leg or shoulder, cut into 1½" pieces)

1" cinnamon stick *(dalchini)*

2 green cardamoms (*chhoti illaichi*)

2 onions - thinly sliced

1 tsp ginger paste

2 tsp garlic paste

½ tsp turmeric (*haldi*) powder

1 tsp red chilli powder

6 tbsp oil

1 tsp salt

1. Heat oil in a pressure cooker. Add the cinnamon stick and cardamoms. Wait for a minute. Add the onions and fry for 8-10 minutes on medium heat till golden brown.
2. Add ginger and garlic paste and stir for 1-2 minutes. Add salt, turmeric powder, chilli powder and meat pieces. Fry on medium flame stirring constantly for 5-7 minutes till the mutton turns glossy and has a well fried look.
3. Add ¾ cup water, give 1 whistle and simmer for 10 minutes. Remove from fire and let the pressure drop by itself.
4. Remove lid and check meat for doneness. Dry away any excess water on fire till oil floats on the surface of mutton. Serve hot.

Ande ka Khagina

Masala scrambled eggs, which go well with paranthas.

Serves 2-3

4 eggs

1 large onion - chopped finely, 1 tsp ginger-garlic paste

¼ tsp turmeric (*haldi*) powder , ½ tsp red chilli powder

2-3 tbsp chopped green coriander, 2 tbsp chopped mint leaves

1-2 green chillies - chopped finely

3-4 tbsp oil, ½ tsp salt, or to taste

1. Beat eggs in a deep bowl. Keep aside.
2. Heat oil in a frying pan or a kadhai. Add onions and fry till golden brown. Add ginger-garlic paste, turmeric and red chilli powder. Stir.
3. Add green chillies, coriander and mint. Stir for a few seconds. Add salt.
4. Add beaten eggs and stir continuously till the eggs turn dry. Check salt. Serve.

Boote ka Kheema

Minced meat with fresh green grams

Serves 4

250 gm mutton mince (*keema*)

250 gm green grams *(boote* or *chholia)*

3 onions - thinly sliced

1 tsp ginger paste, 1 tsp garlic paste

¼ tsp turmeric powder, 1 tsp red chilli powder, 1 tsp salt or to taste

3 green chillies - finely chopped

¼ cup green coriander - chopped

10 fresh mint leaves- chopped

2 tbsp lemon juice

¼ cup oil

1. Heat oil in a *kadahi*. Add onions and stir till golden brown.
2. Add ginger and garlic, cook for 1-2 minutes. Add salt, turmeric, chilli powder, green chillies, coriander and mint.
3. Add mince and fry for about 7-8 minutes till the liquid dries up and separates out as granules. Cook the keema nicely, scraping the sides in between.
4. Add the green gram and ½ tsp salt. Mix well for a minute. Add ½ cup water and cook uncovered for 10-15 minutes on medium flame until mutton is tender.
5. Continue cooking till the excess water dries up. Remove from fire. Squeeze in the lemon juice and serve hot.

Dum ka Murgh

Black cumin, cloves and green cardamoms scent the chicken cooked in a green chilli and yogurt blend.

Serves 4-6

800 gm chicken with bones or 10 drumsticks (lower legs) of chicken

3 medium size onions - thinly sliced

1½ cup yogurt - whisk till very smooth, 1-1½ tsp salt, ¼ tsp turmeric (*haldi*) powder

¼ cup oil

GRIND TOGETHER

10 green chillies - chopped

1 tsp chopped ginger, 1 tbsp chopped garlic

1 tbsp water melon seeds (*magaz*), 5-6 almonds - blanched and chopped

¼ cup yogurt

CRUSH TOGETHER

1 tsp black cumin (*shah jeera*), 4 cloves (*laung*)

2 green cardamoms (*chhoti illaichi*)

1. Grind together green chillies, ginger, garlic, watermelon seeds and almonds with ¼ cup curd till very smooth. Whisk the remaining curd, salt and turmeric with a hand-whisk till very smooth.
2. Wash and pat dry chicken. Add the green chilli paste and the whisked yogurt. Mix well. Marinate the chicken for 1-2 hours in this mixture. Keep in fridge.
3. Heat oil in a heavy based pan and add onions. Cook for 8-10 minutes till golden brown.
4. Now add marinated chicken in it and cook for about 7-8 minutes till the oil separates. Do not cover while cooking. Add enough water and cook for 3-4 minutes or till the chicken is tender.
5. When the chicken is ready, add the crushed spices and cover the kadhai for the flavours to be absorbed by the chicken.

Mutton-Bhindi ka Shorva

A thin and soupy curry with a vegetable invariably added to it. The shorva has an attractive red colour. A few marrow bones are a must in the making of all shorvas.

Serves 4-5

½ kg mutton - cut into medium size pieces

250 gm okra (*bhindi*) - wash, pat dry and slice off the head

1 big lemon size ball of tamarind - soaked in 1 cup hot water for 15 minutes

3 onions - thinly sliced

½ tsp ginger paste, ½ tsp garlic paste

1 tsp red chilli powder

¼ tsp turmeric powder, 1½ tsp salt

2 tbsp yogurt, whisked till smooth

a pinch of garam masala powder

¼ cup green coriander chopped

¼ cup oil

1. Soak tamarind in about 1 cup water for 15 minutes. Deseed, mash and strain to get tamarind water. Keep aside.
2. Slice the head off the okra. Heat oil for deep frying. Fry the okra lightly, retaining the green colour. Keep aside.
3. Heat ¼ cup oil in a pressure cooker, fry the onions on medium heat till golden brown. Put in the ginger and garlic and fry for 1-2 minutes. Add salt, turmeric and red chilli powder. Sprinkle a little water for the spices to blend well. Stir.
4. Add mutton and fry for 5-7 minutes. Add 1½ cups water and pressure cook, till the meat is tender. It takes about 2-3 whistles and then 10 minutes on medium flame for the mutton to get done.
5. Let the pressure drop by itself. When the mutton is cooked properly, add half of the tamarind water, yogurt, deep fried okra and a little additional water, if needed and bring the dish to a boil. Cook covered on slow fire till the okra is cooked through. Check the sourness of the shorva and add more tamarind water as needed. Bring to a boil. Sprinkle garam masala and serve hot.

Achaar Murgh

Achaar Murgh (chicken cooked in pickle style) which is piquant, aromatic and pickle-like, though not necessarily hot. The meat cooks in its own juices, in the fragrance of spices, with no tenderizer and not a drop of water.

Serves 6-8

1 kg chicken (buy 3-4 breast pieces and 6 drumsticks, cut breast into 2" pieces and keep drumsticks whole)

1 tbsp ginger paste and 1½ tbsp garlic paste

4 tsp red chilli powder, 2 tsp cumin (*jeera*) powder, 1½ tsp coriander (*dhania*) powder

10-12 tbsp lemon juice (juice of 3 lemons)

6 green chillies - cut into half lengthwise, ¼ cup chopped curry leaves

2 tsp salt or to taste

TEMPERING (*BAGHAAR*)

2 tsp cumin (*jeera*) seeds, ½ tsp nigella seeds (*kalonji*), 6 dry red chillies

1 tsp mustard seeds (*rai*), 1 tsp fenugreek seeds (*methi dana*)

4-5 tbsp oil

1. Wash and pat dry chicken to drain out the water completely. Place the chicken in a deep bowl and add all the ingredients except the ones for baghaar. Keep the marinated chicken aside for 1 hour.
2. Heat oil in a kadhai. Add cumin, mustard seeds, nigella and fenugreek seeds. Add whole red chillies. When the colour of the red chillies darken, remove from fire. Add the marinated chicken. Mix well.
3. Return the kadhai to heat. First cook chicken on high flame, stirring continuously for 3-4 minutes till it turns whitish on all sides. Cover and cook on medium-slow fire for about 5-7 minutes or till chicken gets tender and the water dries up. Stir once or twice in between. Serve hot.

Shahi Korma

Serves 6-8

1 kg mutton - cut into 1½" pieces

4 onions - finely chopped or grated (2½ cups)

15-20 flakes garlic

1 tsp turmeric (*haldi*) powder, salt to taste

1½ tsp red chili powder, 1½ cups yogurt

1 cup oil or ghee

1 cup cream (optional)

CRUSH TOGETHER

2 small blades of mace (*javetri*), seeds of 6-8 green cardamoms (*chhoti illaichi*)

6 cloves (*laung*), ¼ tsp saffron (*kesar*)

2 tsp ruh kewra

GRIND TOGETHER

1½ tbsp coriander seeds (*saboot dhania*), 24 peppercorns (*saboot kali mirch*)

2" piece ginger

1. Grind garlic flakes with ½ cup water.
2. Grind saboot dhania, ginger and kali mirch to a paste. Keep aside.
3. Crush javetri, seeds of chhoti illaichi, laung and kesar. Add ruh kewra.
4. Heat the oil/ghee, fry the grated onions till golden brown.
5. Add garlic paste, cover the pan and cook for 5 minutes.
6. Add mutton, haldi, salt and lightly beaten yogurt. Cover and cook till the liquid dries.
7. Bhuno mutton for 7-8 minutes till golden brown.
8. Add red chilli powder and coriander seed-ginger-kali mirch paste.
9. Add 2 cups of hot water. Cover and cook on slow fire till the mutton becomes tender or pressure cook on high flame for 7 minutes and then reduce flame and cook for 5 minutes.
10. Add crushed ingredients and cream to the cooked mutton. Leave it over very slow fire for about 10-15 minutes.
11. Serve hot with steamed rice, chappati or nan.

Haleem

A savoury porridge of ground meat and cracked wheat. The roadside eateries all over the city, are seen offering Haleem for iftar, when the day-long fast is formally broken. The word Haleem means mild and the dish is gentle on the system, especially after a day-long fast.

Serves 5-6

1 cup cracked wheat (*dalia*)

500 gm boneless mutton - cut into 1" pieces

4 large onions - thinly sliced

½ tsp ginger paste, 1 tsp garlic paste

¼ tsp turmeric (*haldi)* powder, 1 tsp red chilli powder, 1½ tsp salt, or to taste

1 cup yogurt, whisked

6-7 tbsp oil

¼ tsp garam masala, 4-5 tbsp lemon juice

2 green chillies - finely chopped, a few mint leaves

1. Boil dalia in about 2 cups water till soft. Strain the excess water if any. Cool the dalia in the strainer to drain off all the water. Grind in mixer. Keep aside.
2. Heat oil in a pressure cooker. Add onions and cook for 5-7 minutes till light brown. Remove half the onions and keep aside.
3. Add ginger-garlic paste to the remaining onions and cook for 1-2 minutes. Add salt, chilli powder and turmeric powder, sprinkle a little water & cook for a minute.
4. Add meat and fry well till the liquid dries up. Add ½ cup water and yogurt and pressure cook to allow 2-3 whistles. Reduce heat and keep on slow fire for 10 minutes for the meat to get tender. Let the pressure drop by itself.
5. Open the cooker and cook for 5-6 minutes on high flame till all the moisture is absorbed by the mutton.
6. Cool and grind the cooked meat in mixer.
7. Add ground meat mixture to the ground wheat and cook on medium heat for 5-10 minutes. Add the garam masala and lemon juice. Garnish with fried onions, finely chopped green chillies and fresh mint leaves. Serve hot.

Machchli ka Saalan

This fish curry has a medium thick gravy which is spiced with red chillies and toned with coconut milk.

Serves 4

500 gm boneless fish - cut into 3" pieces

2 medium onions - sliced finely

1½ tsp salt, or to taste, ½ tsp red chilli powder

½ tsp grated ginger, 1 tsp crushed garlic

2 medium tomatoes - blanched, peeled and chopped

½-1 cup coconut milk

6-8 tbsp oil

GRIND TO PASTE

1 tbsp tamarind - deseeded, washed and soaked in ¼ cup water for 15 minutes

1 dry whole red chilli - break into pieces

3 tsp coriander seeds, 1 tsp cumin seeds

¼ tsp turmeric (*haldi*) powder

1. Put the tamarind along with the water in which it is soaked in a small spice grinder. Add red chilli, coriander, cumin and turmeric. Grind to a paste.
2. Heat oil in a kadhai. Add sliced onions cook for 8-10 minutes on medium flame till golden brown. Add ginger, garlic, salt and red chilli powder. Cook for 1 minute, then add the ground spices and fry for 1-2 minutes. Sprinkle 4 tbsp water, cover and simmer for 2-3 minutes for the spices to blend well.
3. Add the chopped tomatoes and cook for 8-10 minutes till the liquid dries up and the tomatoes blend with other spices.
4. Add about 1 cup of water. When the water starts to boil, add the fish fillets. Cover and simmer for 3-4 minutes, stirring occasionally very gently, till the fish is cooked.
5. Reduce heat. Add the coconut milk and simmer on low heat for 1 minute till heated through. Serve hot.

Kali Mirch ka Murgh

This dish has all the aroma and taste of freshly ground peppercorn but is mildly hot.

Serves 4

1 chicken - cut into 8 or 12 pieces

2 medium onions - finely sliced

2 medium onions - ground

1 tsp ginger paste, 1 tsp garlic paste

1 tsp salt, or to taste

1 tbsp freshly ground peppercorns (*sabut kali mirch*)

¼ tsp turmeric (*haldi*) powder

2 tbsp vinegar

8 tbsp oil

1. Mix salt, pepper, turmeric, ginger, garlic and vinegar with the chicken. Marinate for at least 2-3 hours or longer in the refrigerator.
2. Heat oil in a kadhai and fry the sliced onions till light golden. Add the ground onions and fry till golden brown.
3. Add the marinated chicken and stir-fry till the water dries up.
4. Add about ¾ cup water and cook covered on medium fire for about 15 minutes till done.
5. Uncover the pan and cook till dry and the oil comes on top. Sprinkle some freshly crushed peppercorns and serve hot.

Bhuna Keema

Serves 4

½ kg minced mutton

3 medium onions - sliced, 1 tsp ginger paste, 1 tsp garlic paste

1 tsp salt, or to taste, ¼ tsp turmeric powder, 1 tsp red chilli powder

4 tbsp chopped green coriander, 2 tbsp chopped mint leaves

4 green chillies - chopped, 3-4 tbsp lemon juice, 5-6 tbsp oil

1. Heat oil. Fry the onions until golden brown
2. Add ginger and garlic and stir for a minute.
3. Add salt, turmeric, chilli powder and chopped coriander, mint and green chillies. Fry for a couple of minutes.
4. Add the mince. Fry until the mince juices dry up. Add a little water, cover and continue cooking until the mince is tender. Dry any excess water.
5. Squeeze the lemon juice over the meat, and garnish with some coriander, mint and green chillies. Serve hot.

Dalcha

This mutton lentil curry is a Hyderabadi speciality which is lightly soured with tamarind. The lentils absorb the taste of the mutton with which they are cooked.

Serves 6

½ kg mutton

¾ cup split red lentils (*dhuli masoor dal*)

2 tsp melon seeds (*magaz*) - crush or grind in mixer

2 medium onions - thinly sliced, 1 tsp ginger paste, 1½ tsp garlic paste

1 tsp red chilli powder, ½ tsp turmeric (*haldi)* powder, ½ tsp black cumin (*shah jeera*)

½" cinnamon stick (*dalchini*), 2 green cardamoms (*illaichi*), 4 cloves (*laung*)

1 lemon size ball of tamarind - soaked in ½ cup hot water for 15 minutes & strained

½ cup chopped green coriander, 2 green chillies - keep whole

¼ cup oil, 2 tsp salt or to taste

TEMPERING (*BAGHAAR*)

4 dry red chillies, 15-20 curry leaves, 4 tbsp finely chopped garlic

½ tsp cumin seeds (*jeera*), 1 tsp fenugreek seeds (*methi dana*), 2 tbsp oil

1. Pressure cook lentils in 2 cups of water with ½ tsp salt and ¼ tsp turmeric powder to give 1 whistle. Remove from fire and let the pressure drop by itself.
2. Heat oil in a pressure cooker, add black cumin seeds, cinnamon, cloves and cardamom. Cook for 1 minute till spices darken a little. Add onions and cook on medium flame till light brown, add ginger and garlic and cook for 1 minute. Add salt, turmeric, red chilli powder and the ground melon seeds, fry for a few seconds, sprinkle a little water and cook for 1-2 minutes till well blended.
3. Add meat and fry for 6-8 minutes on medium flame till the water dries up and the meat acquires a well fried look. Add ¾-1 cup water for the meat to become tender and pressure cook first on high flame till pressure develops for 2-3 minutes and then reduce heat. Keep on medium flame for 6-8 minutes or till the meat is tender. Remove from fire and wait for the pressure to drop by itself. Check meat for tenderness.
4. Add the prepared boiled lentils, tamarind water, green chillies and coriander and simmer for about 5-7 minutes. Transfer to a serving dish.
5. For baghaar, heat oil. Add all the ingredients of the baghaar. When the red chillies darken, add the baghaar to the hot dalcha. Cover immediately. Serve hot.

Nihari

The word Nihar means fasting. Nihari gosht is cooked overnight and is available at dawn at several roadside eateries in Hyderabad, especially during the holy month of Ramadan, when the Muslims take it during sehri, before dawn. What makes it special and uniquely Hyderabadi is the potli ka masala - a mixture of fragrant herbs and spices, including sandalwood powder, dried rose petals, vetiver roots, galingale roots, bay leaves, etc., which are tied in a cloth potli or bundle, and dipped in the dish when it is simmering.

Serves 4-6

800 gm mutton

1 large onion - sliced finely, 2 large onions - ground to a paste

½ tsp ginger paste, ½ tsp garlic paste, 1 tsp salt, or to taste, ¼ tsp turmeric powder

1 tsp red chilli powder, a few sprigs of green coriander, chopped

10-15 mint leaves, chopped, 2 green chillies, broken into pieces

1½ cups yogurt - whisked till smooth

1 tsp watermelon seeds and 1 tsp musk-melon seeds - ground, 3-4 tbsp lemon juice

¼ cup oil, 2 tbsp potli ka masala tied in a muslin cloth, recipe given below

1. Pressure cook mutton with 2 cups water to give 3-4 whistles. Keep on low heat for 5 minutes. Remove from fire. Let the pressure drop by itself. The mutton should be almost tender.
2. Heat oil. Fry the sliced onions till very light golden. Add the ground onions and fry till golden brown. Add ginger and garlic and fry a minute. Add salt, turmeric and red chilli powder, green coriander, mint and green chillies. Mix well.
3. Add the boiled mutton. Fry for 2-3 minutes. Add yogurt. Stir constantly and fry till the oil comes on top. Add the ground watermelon and musk-melon seeds. Add the mutton stock and an additional 2-3 cups of water. Add 2 tbsp potli ka masala tied in a cloth. Cook on low heat for about 15 minutes, covered. Finally, add lemon juice and the balance of coriander, mint and green chillies. Remove potli. Serve.

POTLI KA MASALA

200 gm coriander seeds, 25 gm sandalwood powder, 35 gm khus, 35 gm bay leaves

20 gm rose petals (dried), 25 gm black cardamom, 30 gm cassia buds

15 gm cinnamon, 30 gm lichen or stoneflower (*pathar ka phool*)

35 gm galingale (*pan ke jadi*), 25 gm gebunwala, 25 gm kapur kachri

Mix these spices and herbs in the given proportions. Store in an air tight jar.

Dahi Murgh

A semi-dry white chicken in a yogurt sauce.

Serves 6

1 chicken (800 gm-1 kg) - cut into 8 or 12 pieces

4 cups yogurt - beaten well till smooth

1½ tsp salt, 1 tsp red chilli powder, ¼ tsp turmeric powder

10 green cardamoms (*illaichi*) - open them slightly, 10 cloves (*laung*), 8 tbsp oil

1. Add salt, turmeric, red chilli powder and chicken to the yogurt. Mix and keep it aside for at least 30 minutes or more.
2. Heat oil. Add cardamoms and cloves. After a few seconds, add the marinated chicken with the yogurt and stir well. Cook on high flame till it starts to boil. Reduce heat and cook on low heat without covering for about 20-25 minutes or till the chicken is tender and oil surfaces.

RICE DISHES

Kachche Gosht ki Biryani

Serves 6

2 cups basmati rice - wash and soak for 15 minutes

5 large onions - slice finely and deep fried till crisp and brown

MARINATE TOGETHER

1 kg lamb - cut into ¾" pieces, wash, pat dry, 2 cups yogurt

1 tbsp ginger paste, 2 tbsp garlic paste, 2 green chillies - chopped

¼ cup chopped fresh pudina, 2 tsp red chilli powder, 1 tsp haldi, 1½ tsp salt

RICE

4-6 cloves (*laung*), 1" stick cinnamon (*dalchini*), 5 green cardamoms (*illaichi*)

1 black cardamom, 10 saboot kali mirch, ½ tsp shah jeera, 1 tsp salt

OTHER INGREDIENTS

1" piece ginger - cut into juliennes, ½ tsp cardamom powder, 2 tsp garam masala

2 tbsp chopped coriander, 2-3 tbsp whole mint leaves, 6 tbsp ghee - melted

a few strands saffron mixed in ¼ cup warm milk, 2 tbsp fresh rose petals

1 tsp rose water, 1 tsp kewra water, dough (made of atta) to seal

1. Mix yogurt, ginger and garlic paste, chopped green chillies, red chilli powder, turmeric powder, salt, one-third of the fried sliced onions and chopped mint leaves. Add mutton and mix. Marinate for 6-8 hours or overnight in the fridge.
2. For rice, boil 5 cups of water. Add 1 tsp salt, shah jeera. Tie the remaining spices in a muslin cloth and tie up in a potli. Add this potli to the boiling water. Add rice. Bring to a boil and cook rice for 5 minutes till partly done, about 70% done. Drain and spread out on a tray.
3. Grease the bottom of a thick bottomed handi or an oven proof dish. Arrange half of the mutton. Over it arrange half of the parboiled rice. Then arrange one-third of the fried sliced onions and ginger juliennes. Sprinkle half of the cardamom powder, garam masala powder and chopped coriander and mint.
4. Pour 3 tbsp ghee on top. Warm milk and dissolve saffron in it. Add half the saffron milk to the biryani. Sprinkle half rose petals, rose water and kewra water.
5. Repeat layers once again. Cover the vessel with a lid. Seal the lid with flour dough. Place a tawa on high flame. Keep the handi on the tawa for 3-4 minutes on high heat. Reduce heat and cook on low heat on the tawa for 45 minutes. If using an oven proof dish, cover with foil and keep in a warm oven at 150°C for 45 minutes. Remove from fire. Check mutton for doneness. Mix lightly. Serve.

Dumpukht Biryani

Rice and mutton are partially cooked and then layered in a deep handi. Moistened with milk, they are then cooked to perfection in the sealed handi kept on very low heat.

Serves 8

1 kg mutton - cut into small pieces

3 cups basmati rice - boil with ½ tsp turmeric added to the water

4 onions - ground to a paste in the mixer, 2 tsp ginger paste

2" piece of raw green papaya - grate with the peel and grind to a paste with just a little water (use only 1 tsp green papaya paste for the recipe), 2 cups yogurt

a few threads of saffron (*kesar*), ½ cup ghee (clarified butter) or oil, 2 bay leaves (*tej patta*)

1 black cardamom (*moti illaichi*), 8 green cardamoms (*chhoti illaichi*)

1" stick cinnamon (*dalchini*), 8-10 peppercorns (*sabut kali mirch*), 1½ tsp red chilli powder

½ tsp turmeric (*haldi*), 2 tsp coriander (*dhania*) powder, salt to taste, ½ cup milk

GRIND SPICES TOGETHER

1 tsp peppercorns (*sabut kali mirch*), ½ tsp cumin seeds (*jeera*), 6 cloves (*laung*)

seeds of 2 black cardamoms (*moti illaichi*)

1. Wash mutton. Pat dry on a kitchen towel to drain out all water. Add 1½ tsp salt, a little saffron, onion paste, ginger paste and just 1 tsp papaya paste to the mutton. Rub the mixture well into the meat. Add the yogurt and the freshly ground spices. Set aside for at least 4-5 hours or overnight in the fridge.
2. Take a heavy-bottomed pan and heat oil or ghee in it. Add bay leaves, black cardamom, 1" stick cinnamon, peppercorns and green cardamoms. Wait for a minute for the spices to turn fragrant. Add the marinated mutton along with the marinade and stir continuously on high heat for 3-4 minutes. Add red chilli powder, turmeric, and coriander powder. Mix well. Cover and cook on low medium heat for about 20 minutes, stirring occasionally till mutton is almost cooked. Check salt and masalas and adjust to taste.
3. Take a handi or an oven-proof dish. Grease with oil. Put 1/3 of rice. Top with half the mutton. Again put half of the remaining rice and cover with the left over mutton. Top with rice. Sprinkle the milk on the rice. Cover the pan with a tight fitting lid or aluminium foil. Seal it with dough. Place the handi on a tawa on high heat for 5-7 minutes and then reduce heat and keep for 20-25 minutes so that the meat gets tender and the rice is done.

Seviyon ki Biryani

Vermicelli pilaf with mutton

Serves 4

250 gm thin, long vermicelli

½ kg mutton - cut into medium pieces

milk of one coconut or 1½ cups ready-made coconut milk

3 medium onions - finely sliced, 1 tsp ginger paste, 1 tsp garlic paste

2-3 green chillies - chopped, ¼ tsp turmeric powder, 1 tsp red chilli powder

¼ cup chopped fresh green coriander, ¼ cup chopped fresh mint

½ cup yogurt - whisked, 3-4 tbsp lemon juice, ¼ cup oil, ¼ cup ghee

GRIND TOGETHER

½" piece cinnamon stick (*dalchini*), 4 green cardamoms (*illaichi*)

4 cloves (*laung*), ½ tsp peppercorn (*kali mirch*), ½ tsp black cumin (*shah jeera*)

1. Heat 1 tbsp of oil/ghee. Stir fry the vermicelli for about 4-5 minutes on medium fire, till golden brown. Keep aside.
2. For the coconut milk, grate coconut. Mix 1½ cups of warm water. Strain through a muslin to get coconut milk. Discard the residue and keep milk aside.
3. Heat ¼ cup oil and ¼ cup ghee in a pressure cooker. Add the onions and fry till golden brown. Add ginger and garlic and the green chillies. Stir to mix well.
4. Add salt, turmeric, red chilli powder and chopped coriander and mint.
5. Add meat and stir fry for 5 minutes. Add yogurt and fry till the liquid somewhat dries up. Add just enough water (about 1 cup) for the meat to get cooked. Pressure cook the meat on high flame to give 4-5 whistles and then keep on low heat for 5-7 minutes. Remove from fire and let the pressure drop by itself. Check that the mutton is tender.
6. Transfer the mutton to a wide flat pan or a large kadhai. Add the coconut milk to the meat. Keep on fire. Do not allow to bring to a boil. Add the vermicelli. Mix gently. Sprinkle some coriander and mint and the ground spices.
7. Add the juice of lemon evenly on top. Cover and cook over medium-slow heat till the vermicelli is cooked. Take care to see that strands of vermicelli stay apart and do not get mushy. Serve hot.

Doodh ki Biryani

Mutton pilaf in milk flavoured with herbs and spices.

Serves 4

2 cups rice

500 gm mutton (chops, marrow bones and medium sized pieces on the bone)

2 cups milk, 1 cup water

2 tbsp ghee, 1 tsp salt, or to taste

POTLI -1

2 onions - sliced

½ tsp ginger - grated, ½ tsp coarsely ground garlic

POTLI -2

5 green chillies - chopped

¼ cup chopped fresh green coriander, ¼ cup chopped fresh mint

POTLI - 3

1 tsp caraway seeds

1" piece of cinnamon, 4 green cardamoms, 4 cloves

1. Boil a large panful of water (10-12 cups). Add 2 tsp salt to the boiling water. Add rice and stir to mix well. Boil till 80% cooked (soft, yet chewy). Strain. Leave in the strainer for a minute and then spread on a tray.
2. Tie the ingredients of all the 3 potlis separately in three squares of muslin cloth.
3. Pressure cook mutton with all the 3 potlis, salt, milk and water to give 4 whistles. Reduce heat and keep on low heat for 5 minutes. Let the pressure drop by itself. Check that meat is tender. Squeeze out the liquids from the pouches. Take care to leave the rice a little wet, just adequate to allow the par-boiled rice to get fully cooked.
4. Take a heavy-bottomed handi or a deep pan. Brush the bottom with little ghee. Put meat and rice and mix them in the pan. Dot the surface with ghee. Cover with a tight fitting lid or aluminium foil.
5. Keep the handi on a hot tawa for 5 minutes on medium heat. Reduce heat and let the rice cook on low heat for 10 minutes till it cooked and steaming hot.

Hyderabadi Biryani Khaas

Rice and chicken are cooked separately, and then they are layered together along with fried onions. The pot is tightly sealed and steamed on low heat to allow all the flavours to blend.

Serves 6-8

RICE

2 cups uncooked long grain basmati rice, 1 tbsp oil, 2 bay leaves (*tej patta*), 1½ tsp salt

FOR THE CHICKEN

1 chicken (700-800 gm) - cut into 12 pieces

4 large onions - chopped, 1½ tbsp ginger-garlic paste, 2 large tomatoes - chopped

1 cup thick yogurt (*curd*), 5-6 tbsp oil, 1 tsp red chilli powder, salt to taste

GARNISHING

1 cup sliced onions - fried till crisp and brown (2-3 large onions), ½ cup mint leaves

few strands saffron (*kesar*) soaked in 1 tsp water and 2 drops kewra essence

FLAVOURING MASALA

1½ tsp cumin (*jeera*), 3-4 green cardamoms (*chhoti illaichi*), 2" cinnamon (*dalchini*)

2 black cardamoms (*moti illaichi*), 2-3 peppercorns (*saboot kali mirch*), 3-4 cloves (*laung*)

1. To cook the rice, boil 7 cups of water with tej patta, salt, and oil. Add the rice and cook till almost tender. Strain and spread the drained rice on a wide tray. Run a fork through the rice to let the steam escape.
2. For chicken, heat oil in a kadhai/wok. Add onions. Stir fry till brown. Add ginger-garlic paste. Mix well. Add tomatoes. Cook till dry. Add curd. Stir for 1 minute. Add salt, chilli powder and chicken. Bhuno for 8 minutes. Add 1 cup water Cook till tender. Remove from fire.
3. Grind all the ingredients for the flavouring masala in a blender to a paste with ¼ cup water. Strain it through a sieve. Keep liquid masala aside.
4. For assembling the biryani, take a large heavy-bottomed pan, sprinkle some curry of the chicken at the bottom. Spread some of the rice. Place ½ the chicken pieces on it and wet the rice with some curry. Sprinkle some of the fried onion and poodina on it. Sprinkle 2-3 tbsp liquid flavouring masala.
5. Repeat by adding rice, then chicken, followed by poodina and fried onions and flavouring masala. Finish with a top layer of rice sprinkled with fried onions, poodina, flavouring masala and kesar mixture. Mix slightly.
6. Cover pan with a tight fitting lid and seal the lid with dough. Place the pan on fire with a tawa underneath to reduce the heat to minimum for ½ hour before serving.

BREADS

Anda Parantha

Layered bread with egg stuffing.

Makes 4

DOUGH

2 cups whole wheat flour (*atta*)

1 tbsp oil

½ tsp salt

½-¾ cup water for kneading dough

EGG FILLING

2-3 eggs - beat well

½ tsp salt

2 green chillies - finely chopped

1 small onion - finely chopped

4-5 tbsp chopped green coriander

1. For the dough, mix oil and salt with flour. Using a little water knead to make medium soft dough.
2. Whisk the eggs well. Add a little salt, green chillies, onion and coriander. Set filling aside.
3. Take a big onion sized ball of dough. Roll out to a big oblong shape. Spread some oil. Pinch the centre lightly to make a figure of '8', fold over to make one round parantha. Roll out the parantha lightly and place on a hot tawa. When the underside gets done, reduce heat. Open the pinched edge with a knife to form a pocket.
4. Fill some egg mixture and let the parantha cook a little. Turn over and spread ghee. Fry till both sides are crisp and golden. Make all paranthas in the same way.

ACHAAR & CHUTNEY

Gosht ka Achaar

This meat pickle is soured with lemon juice and like most Hyderabadi pickles seasoned with several spices.

Serves 6-8

1 kg boneless mutton - cut into 1½" pieces

2½ tsp salt, 1 tsp turmeric powder (*haldi*), 4 tbsp red chilli powder

½ cup lemon juice, 2 tbsp chopped ginger, oil for frying

DRY ROAST TOGETHER AND GRIND

4 tsp cumin seeds (*jeera*), ½ tsp nutmeg (*jaiphal*)

BAGHAAR

2 tsp cumin seeds

2 tsp black mustard seeds, 6-7 green cardamoms

8-9 cloves, 7-8 whole dry red chillies, 20-25 curry leaves, 4-5 tbsp oil

1. Boil the meat pieces with salt till tender. Deep fry for a minute in oil. Do not fry for long as the meat might get chewy.
2. Drain the water. Soak in lemon juice with ginger pieces overnight. Next morning, add the roasted and ground spices, turmeric and chilli powder.
3. Heat oil. Add the spices for baghaar, with curry leaves last of all. When the spices darken a little, pour the baghaar into the meat.
4. When cool, transfer to a dry, clean, airtight jar.

Note

Prawn, chicken, quail and partridge pickle can also be made the same way.

DESSERTS

Khubani ka Meetha

Pulp of apricot with cream. Traditionally the light brown apricots with the seed are used. The kernel of the seed is used as the garnish for the dessert. Here we have used the orange, seedless variety of apricots to make the pulp and garnished with blanched and slivered almonds.

Serves 8-10

½ kg dried apricot (*khubani*)

¾ cup (150 gm) sugar, or to taste, 250 gm fresh cream

GARNISH

almonds

1. Soak apricots overnight with ¼ cup sugar in 2 cups water to cover them.
2. Next morning, boil apricots in the same water till tender. Remove seeds if present.
3. Sieve till only the fibre remains in the strainer.
4. Add a little water, the remaining sugar and cook till you get the consistency of custard. Garnish the dish with almonds. Serve with fresh cream.

Khajoor ka Halwa

A halwa of dates with lentils. An unusual dessert inspired from Arabia.

Serves 6-8

½ kg dates

1½ cups split gram lentils (*channe ki dal*)

1½ kg milk

1½ cups clarified butter (*ghee*)

4 tbsp screwpine flower water (*kewra*)

10-15 almonds - blanched, peeled and cut into thin slices

a few pistachios

seeds of 4-5 green cardamoms - crushed

¼ cup sugar, or to taste

1. Wash the gram lentils and put in a kadhai. Add milk and bring to a boil. Boil on low medium heat for about 20 minutes till the lentils are tender and liquids dry up. Remove from fire and let them cool. Grind the lentils to a paste.
2. Wash and deseed dates. Boil in ¼ cup water for 5-6 minutes. Remove from fire and let it cool. Mash the dates with your hands.
3. Mix dates with lentil paste.
4. Heat ghee in a clean heavy bottom kadhai. Add the dates and lentil mixture and fry well. Then add sugar and cook for another few minutes.
5. Add screwpine flower water and crushed cardamoms. Decorate with almonds and pistachio. Serve.

Double ka Meetha

This bread pudding is a Hyderabadi variety of the Shahi Tukri of North India. The name comes from the word double roti, which is the Indian name for bread.

Serves 15-20

10 slices of fresh white bread - remove crust and cut each into half diagonally

½ kg milk

½ cup cream

1 cup sugar, ½ cup water

a pinch of saffron (*kesar*) - soaked in 2 tbsp rose water

¾ cup ghee (clarified butter)

12-15 almonds - blanched and sliced

15 pistachio - sliced

a few sheets of silver leaves (*chandi ke warq*), optional

1. Boil milk. Reduce heat. Cook on medium heat for 10-15 minutes till the consistency is reduced to almost half. Add cream and cook for a minute. Keep aside.
2. Boil sugar in ½ cup water and make syrup. Keep aside to cool. Mix saffron soaked in rose water to sugar syrup.
3. Heat ghee in a pan. Shallow fry the bread slices till light golden on both sides.
4. Brush a baking tray with ghee. Place the bread slices in the tray and soak each slice of bread with about a tbsp of flavoured sugar syrup.
5. Now pour creamy milk on the bread slices. Sprinkle almond and pistachio. Allow the bread to soak in the liquids. Bake in pre-heated oven at 180°C for 15-20 minutes till the liquids almost dry up. Decorate with silver leaves.

Makhane ki Kheer

A dessert of lotus seeds.

Serves 8-10

2 kg milk, 100 gm lotus seeds (*makhane*) - roast for 1-2 minutes in a pan
¾ cup sugar or to taste, ½ tsp green cardamom (*illaichi)* powder
2-3 tbsp screwpine flower (*kewra water),* 1 tbsp chopped green pista

1. Roast the lotus seeds till they start to change colour. Let them cool. Crush half of them, leaving the other half whole.
2. Boil milk. When the milk starts to boil, add the lotus seeds and cook in milk at medium heat, stirring every now and then. Cook till the lotus seeds are cooked and the consistency of the milk reduced by one third.
3. Add sugar and sprinkle crushed cardamom. Cook further for a couple of minutes. Remove from heat.
4. Add kewra water. Transfer to a serving dish. Decorate with silver leaves and chopped pista.

Glossary of Names/Terms

HINDI OR ENGLISH NAMES as used in India	USED IN USA/UK/OTHER COUNTRIES
Baingan	Eggplant, aubergine
Bhutta	Corn
Capsicum	Bell peppers
Chhoti Illaichi	Green cardamom
Chilli powder	Red chilli powder, Cayenne pepper
Cornflour	Cornstarch
Dalchini	Cinnamon
French beans	Green beans
Gobhi	Cauliflower
Hara Dhania	Cilantro/fresh or green coriander leaves
Hari Gobhi	Broccoli
Hari Mirch	Green hot peppers, green chillies
Imli	Tamarind
Jeera	Cumin seeds
Saunf	Fennel
Sela Chaawal	Parboiled rice, which when cooked is not sticky at all
Seviyaan	Vermicelli
Soda-bi-carb	Baking soda
Til	Sesame seeds
Toned Milk	Milk with 1% fat content
Yellow Capsicum	Yellow bell peppers